A Red Fox

by Joaquin Garcia
illustrated by Pat Lucas-Morris

Core Decodable 35

McGraw Hill Education

Bothell, WA • Chicago, IL • Columbus, OH • New York, NY

MHEonline.com

Send all inquiries to:
McGraw-Hill Education
8787 Orion Place
Columbus, OH 43240

ISBN: 978-0-02-144873-9
MHID: 0-02-144873-6

Printed in Canada.

9 10 11 12 KOD 24

A red fox has a den.

Its den is down in grass.

If the sun is down, a red fox hunts.

A red fox can hunt down a rabbit.

A red fox can smell hens.

At sun-up, a red fox rests. It sits down.